GUITAR SPRINGBOARD by Michael Morenga

Technical Workout

Finger-fitness for guitarists

Wise Publications
part of The Music Sales Group
London / New York / Paris / Sydney / Copenhagen / Berlin / Madrid / Tokyo

Published by
Wise Publications
8/9 Frith Street, London, W1D 3JB, England.

Exclusive distributors:
Music Sales Limited
Distribution Centre, Newmarket Road,
Bury St Edmunds, Suffolk, IP33 3YB, England.

Music Sales Pty Limited
120 Rothschild Avenue, Rosebery, NSW 2018, Australia.

Order No. AM984830
ISBN 1-84609-421-6

Translated & edited by Rebecca Taylor.

Printed in the EU.

Your Guarantee of Quality:
As publishers, we strive to produce every book
to the highest commercial standards.

The book has been carefully designed to minimise awkward page turns
and to make playing from it a real pleasure. Particular care has been given
to specifying acid-free, neutral-sized paper made from pulps
which have not been elemental chlorine bleached.

This pulp is from farmed sustainable forests and
was produced with special regard for the environment.

Throughout, the printing and binding have been planned
to ensure a sturdy, attractive publication which should give
years of enjoyment.

If your copy fails to meet our high standards, please inform us
and we will gladly replace it.

www.musicsales.com

Introduction

You will probably have been told hundreds of times that to become a great guitarist you need a great technique! This book therefore aims to teach you a number of tricks you can use to improve your agility on the fretboard and strengthen both hands, helping to make you a better player. As well as providing the perfect starting point for the guitarist wishing to learn the basic techniques from the very beginning, the exercises in this book could even be used as a reference when you become a more advanced player. Let's start by learning about some of the really basic tricks:

● Positioning of the fretted hand

● The picking hand: holding the plectrum, hand position

● Picking techniques: up-strokes and down-strokes, alternate strokes

Hand position

● Keep your wrist straight

● Make sure your fingers are relaxed

Finger position

● Your fingertips should be almost perpendicular to the strings, and your index finger slightly bent to the side

● Arch your fingers over the strings. The palm should not touch the fretboard, regardless of the position

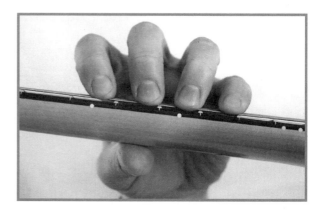

Thumb position

● Your thumb must support the back of the neck, at about the same level as the middle two fingers

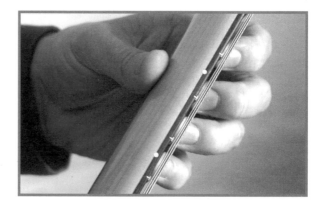

Now let's look in more detail at your finger-position on the fretboard. You will notice that the frets get smaller as you move closer to the body of the guitar and because of this you will have to alter your finger-position as you move.

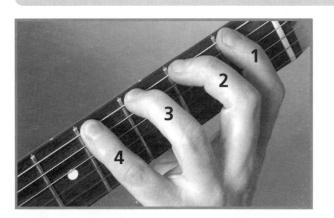

- Position the fingers of your fretted hand directly next to the metal bars of the fretboard

  1 = index finger
  2 = middle finger
  3 = ring finger
  4 = little finger

- The distance between your fingers should correspond to the distance between the frets you are using

- Position your fingers in the centre of the frets, so that they don't rest on the metal bars

The hand positions shown above are only a recommendation. The size of your hand and length of your fingers should be taken into consideration when deciding how to hold the guitar. Whatever position you find is most comfortable, ensure that:

- Any unused fingers do not touch the string of the note being played
- Your thumb position is correct

Tips

Picking hand technique

Holding the plectrum

It is important to hold the plectrum properly so that your picking technique is as neat and rhythmic as possible.

- Rest the plectrum on the inside of your index finger and bend the other fingers in towards the palm
- The thumb should gently rest on the plectrum, holding it in position

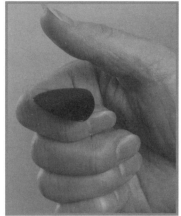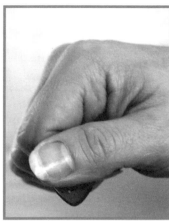

Hand position

- The picking hand should always stay close to the strings when playing
- If you move it too far away you will find it difficult to play fast passages

Strumming motion

- The strumming motion should originate from your wrist, not your fingers or, indeed, your lower arm
- Your wrist should be aligned with your lower arm, and not bent

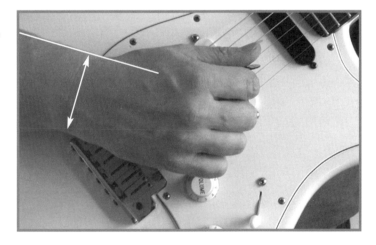

Tips

The hand positions shown above are only a recommendation. The size of your hand and length of your fingers should be taken into consideration when deciding how to hold the guitar. Whatever position you find is most comfortable, ensure that:

- The picking hand is relaxed over the strings
- The thumb only rests gently on the plectrum
- The picking motion originates from the wrist, not from the lower arm

The down-stroke

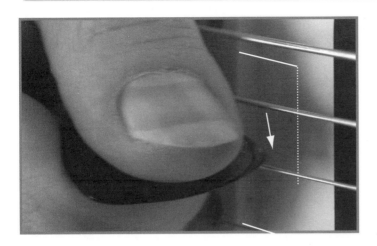

The symbol for a down-stroke is ⊓. It is played as follows:

● Starting just above the string, move your hand in a downwards motion, keeping it parallel to the strings

● The picking radius (total movement of the plectrum) should stay within the two neighbouring strings

The up-stroke

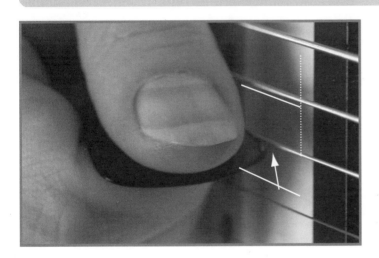

The symbol for an up-stroke is V. It is played as follows:

● Starting just below the string, move your hand in an upwards motion, keeping it parallel to the strings

● The picking radius (total movement of the plectrum) should stay within the two neighbouring strings

Alternate picking

Alternate picking is simply a combination of the down-stroke and up-stroke. It's symbol is ⊓ V.

● This technique is very useful for playing single lines of music

● Its most common form is a down-stroke followed by an up-stroke although it can also appear as an up-stroke followed by a down-stroke

There are four basic picking methods:

● Down-strokes only (⊓ ⊓ ⊓ etc.)

● Up-strokes only (V V V etc.)

● Alternate picking: down-stroke, up-stroke (⊓ V ⊓ V etc.)

● Alternate picking: up-stroke, down-stroke (V ⊓ V ⊓ etc.)

Tips

Positions

'Position' refers to the location of the fingers of the fretted hand. To play in the first position, the index finger should be aligned with the first fret. In order to distinguish positions from fret numbers in musical notation, positions are usually written in roman numerals. Don't confuse these with the roman numerals used to represent scale degrees (☞ *GUITAR SPRINGBOARD: Harmonic Workout*).

In bar 2 beat 1 of exercise 1 below, you will notice that the index finger moves to the fifth fret. The new position is called fifth position.

Exercises 1–6 allow you to work on four important elements of your technique:

● The most basic finger-pattern, 1–2–3–4

● Changing position on every string

● Alternate picking

● Synchronisation of the fretted and picking hands

Low E string

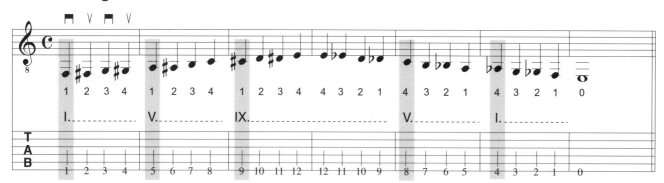

A string

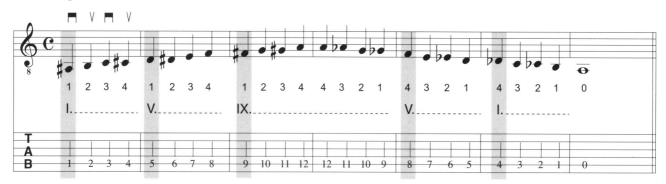

D string

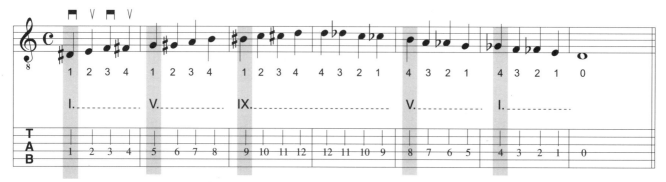

G string

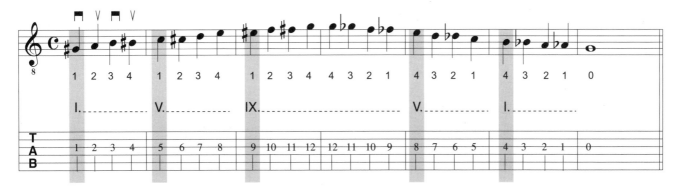

B string

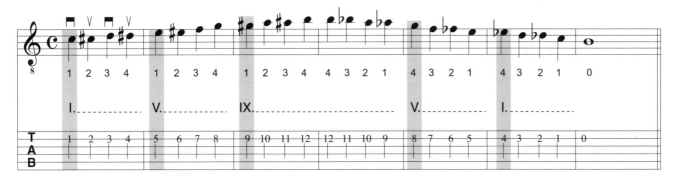

High E string

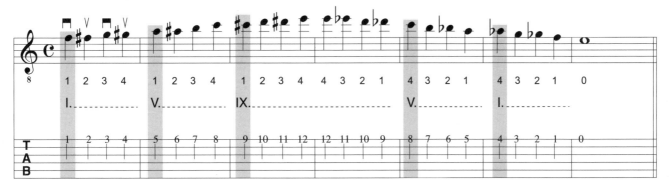

- Practise fret changes slowly in front of a mirror
- After the 12th fret, notes repeat themselves one octave higher. First/13th fret = F, third/15th fret = G etc.
- Practise playing all the notes slowly and confidently. This will help you get to grips with the music quicker
- Practise changing positions with a metronome. This will help your timing
- Record your practice. By listening to your playing you will learn to play with more precision

Tips

Variations

You can play finger-patterns (the most basic pattern being 1–2–3–4) in a variety of different ways on the fretboard. These are called 'variations'.

Three variations are depicted in the following diagram. You should practise these in the following manner.

- Variation 1: play the finger-pattern 1–2–3–4 forwards and backwards on all six strings in the first position

- Variation 2: play the finger-pattern forwards and backwards on all six strings in the second position. Thereafter, play it forwards in the third position and backwards in the fourth position. This way, you can practise the exercise over the entire fretboard

- Variation 3: play the finger-pattern forwards on all six strings starting in the first position, extending it over the entire fretboard. Once you have reached the end of the fretboard, play it in reverse until you arrive back in the first position

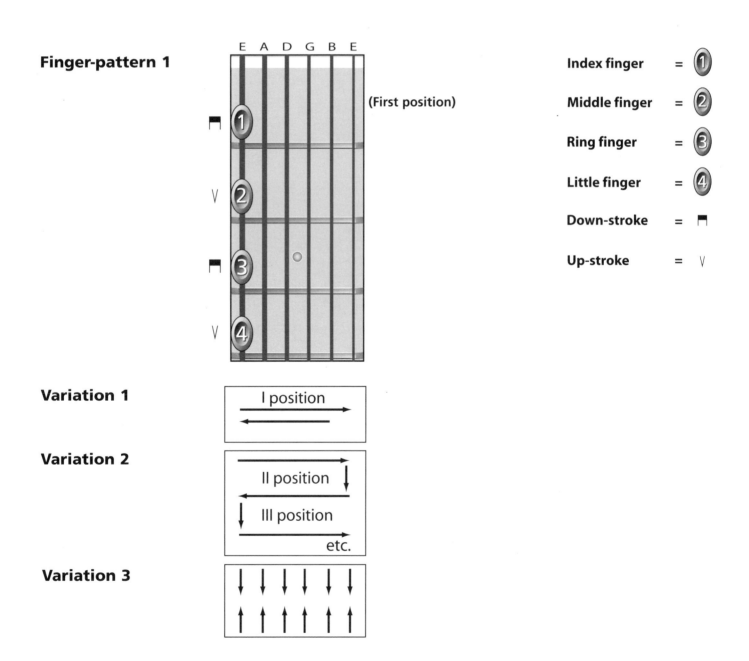

Finger-pattern 1

(First position)

Index finger	=	①
Middle finger	=	②
Ring finger	=	③
Little finger	=	④
Down-stroke	=	⊓
Up-stroke	=	∨

Variation 1

I position

Variation 2

II position
III position
etc.

Variation 3

The basics of a good technique

There are three elements to a good technique:

- Confident movement of the fretted hand

- Good synchronisation of the fretted hand and the picking hand

- Good physical fitness: litheness and independence of all four fingers

The exercises on the following pages aim to help you achieve the technique you will need to be able to play songs proficiently and sight read with ease.

Exercise 1

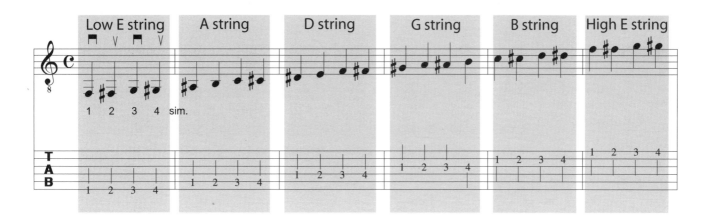

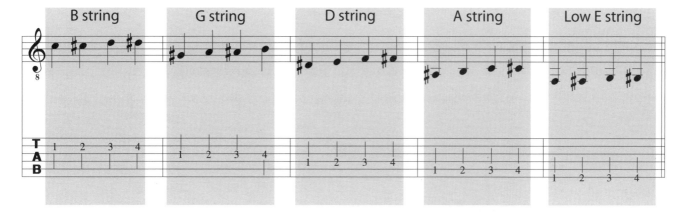

1. Put the index finger of your fretted hand on the first fret on the low E string (as close to the metal bar as possible). Play a down-stroke with the plectrum

2. Put the middle finger of your fretted hand on the second fret. Play an up-stroke with the plectrum. Your index finger should stay on the string

3. Put the ring finger of your fretted hand on the third fret. Play a down-stroke with the plectrum. Your index and middle fingers should stay on the string

4. Put the little finger of your fretted hand on the fourth fret. Play an up-stroke with the plectrum. Your index, middle and ring fingers should stay on the string

5. Remove the four fingers of your fretted hand from the string. Then move your hand to the A string, keeping it parallel to the strings. Repeat steps 1–4 on the A string. Play the exercise in this way over all six strings

Step by step guidance through exercise 1

11

Finger independence and synchronisation

Exercise 2: finger pattern 1: 1–2–3–4 using variation 2

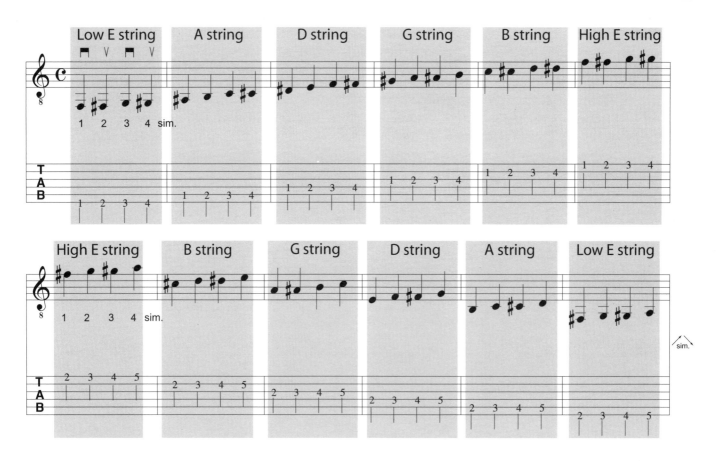

Exercise 3: finger pattern 1: 1–2–3–4 using variation 3 (first to fifth position)

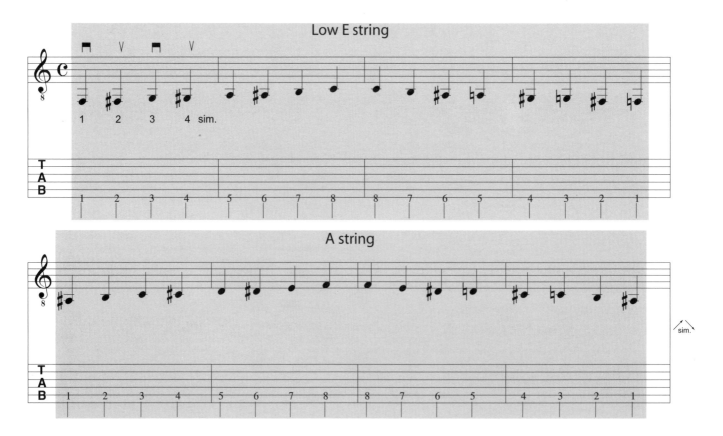

Each finger can be used as a starting finger to produce six different combinations of the 1–2–3–4 finger-pattern. This creates 24 new finger-patterns. These patterns form the basis of the '1000 finger' chart.

Block 1 Finger-pattern	(Start with index finger - 1)			
1	1	2	3	4
2	1	2	4	3
3	1	3	2	4
4	1	3	4	2
5	1	4	2	3
6	1	4	3	2

Block 2 Finger-pattern	(Start with middle finger - 2)			
7	2	1	3	4
8	2	1	4	3
9	2	3	1	4
10	2	3	4	1
11	2	4	1	3
12	2	4	3	1

Block 3 Finger-pattern	(Start with ring finger - 3)			
13	3	1	2	4
14	3	1	4	2
15	3	2	1	4
16	3	2	4	1
17	3	4	1	2
18	3	4	2	1

Block 4 Finger-pattern	(Start with little finger - 4)			
19	4	1	2	3
20	4	1	3	2
21	4	2	1	3
22	4	2	3	1
23	4	3	1	2
24	4	3	2	1

- Start with block 1 (finger-patterns 1–6) and variation 1 (see page 10)

- Train yourself to play problematic finger-patterns perfectly by repeating them slowly and confidently. Your aim should be to play all 24 patterns without making a single mistake!

- Make yourself a practice schedule: for example, learn all five finger-patterns up to the fifth fret to start with. When you can play those, move on

- Record your practice sessions. By listening back to yourself, you will learn to play with more precision

- Experiment with the chart and discover the different possibilities for yourself (e.g. 1–2–3–4, 2–3–4–1, 3–4–2–1)

- All the finger patterns make good warm-up exercises

Tips

13

Extension exercises for the '1000 finger' chart

Here are a few exercises to help you unleash the creative potential of the '1000 finger' chart.

- **Exercise 4:** a different finger-pattern on each string, but using the same starting finger
- **Exercise 5:** one finger-pattern over two strings, two fingers per string
- **Exercise 6:** one finger-pattern alternating over two strings
- **Exercise 7:** one finger-pattern over four strings
- **Exercise 8:** one finger-pattern over four strings with string jumping (missing out one or more strings)

Exercise 4: finger patterns 1–6

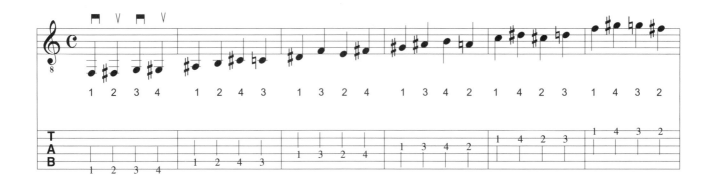

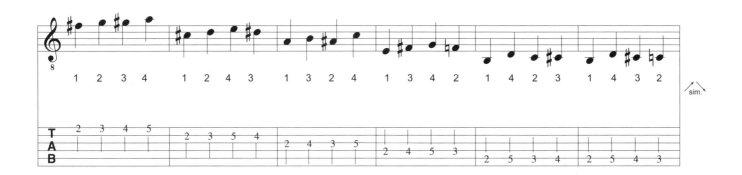

Tips

- Constructing a training program for yourself using the exercises in this book is an effective way to practise
- Practise intensively for short periods at first, then gradually increase your practice time
- To start with, concentrate on small areas of the fretboard and when you have mastered these, incorporate more sections into your routine

Extension exercises for the '1000 finger' chart

Exercise 5: two notes played on one string. Finger-pattern 1

Exercise 6: alternating between two strings. Finger-pattern 1

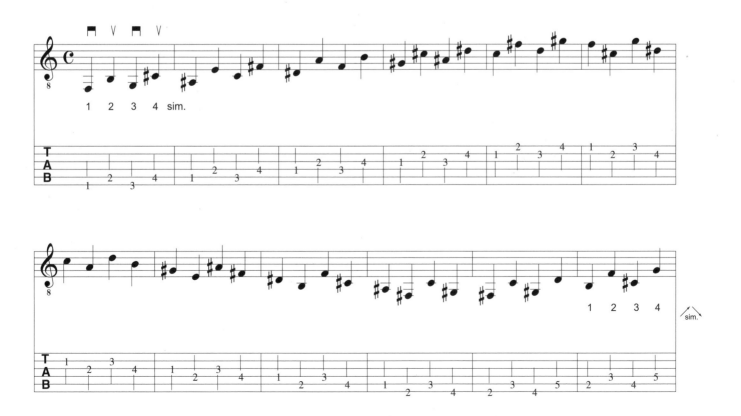

Extension exercises for the '1000 finger' chart

Exercise 7: finger-pattern 1 on four strings (E–A–D–G, A–D–G–B, D–G–B–E)

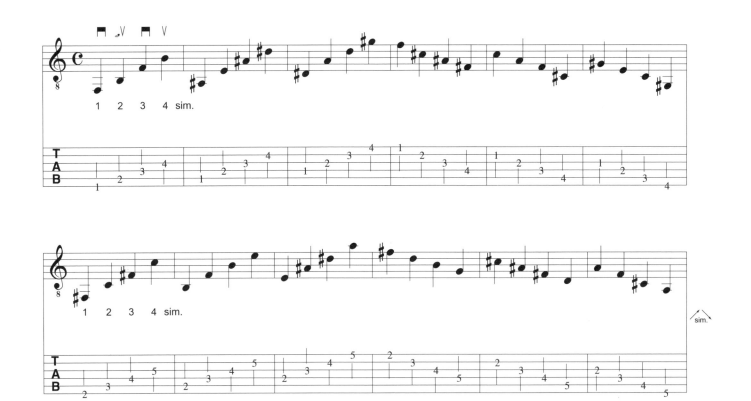

Exercise 8: finger-pattern 1 with string jumping

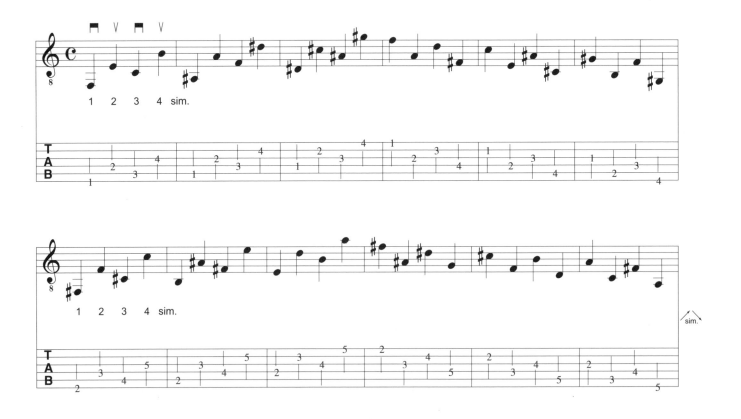

16

The term 'finger-roll' refers to the process of transferring a finger from one string to another without lifting it off the fretboard.

- Forwards finger-roll: by bending the finger it moves to the neighbouring higher string without lifting off the fretboard (☞ photos 1 and 2)

- Backwards finger-roll: the finger is placed on the fretboard with the string roughly aligned as close to the bottom of the nail as possible. Without lifting it is bent or 'rolled' over onto the neighbouring lower string (☞ photos 3 and 4)

| 1: Starting position on E string | 2: Forwards finger-roll (E to A string) | 3: Starting position on e' string | 4: Backwards finger-roll (e' to b string) |

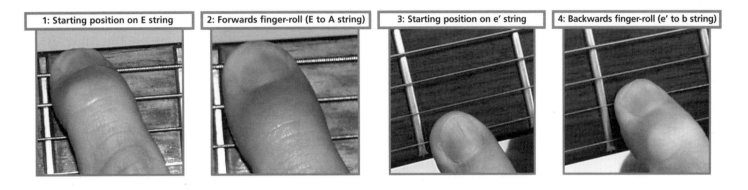

Exercise 9: forwards and backwards finger-rolls using the little finger

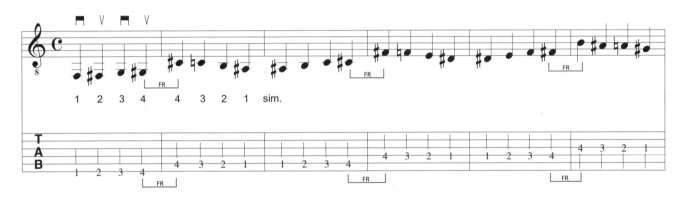

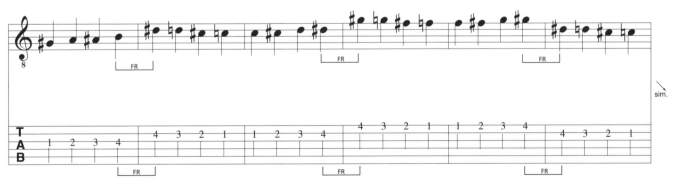

- The finger-roll technique can be used forwards and backwards on all six strings

- You can create exercises for the fretted hand by mixing different finger-patterns together. For example, to strengthen your ring finger, try combining finger-pattern 2 (block 1) with finger-patterns 13–18 (block 3)

- Don't confuse the finger-roll technique with the barré technique (☞ GUITAR SPRINGBOARD: Advanced Harmonic Workout) .

Tips

Finger independence and synchronisation

Exercise 10

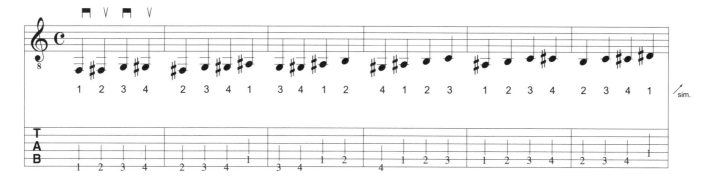

Exercise 11

Exercise 12

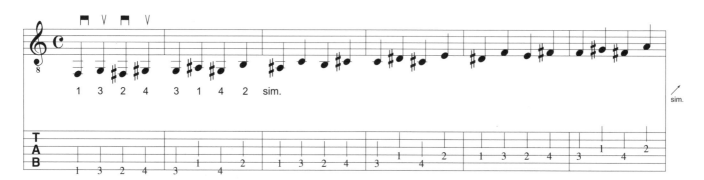

Exercise 13

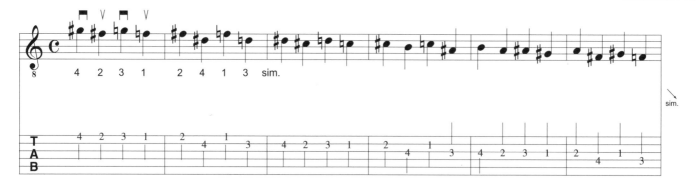

The word 'chromatic' comes from the Greek word 'chroma' meaning colour and refers to a note or group of notes which are outside the key signature (see *GUITAR SPRINGBOARD: Scales Made Easy*). Each chromatic step is the equivalent of one fret on the guitar. When a sequence of chromatic notes is played, we call this 'chromatic motion'.

The following exercises are designed to help you strengthen the fingers of the fretted hand by playing chromatic passages.

Exercise 14

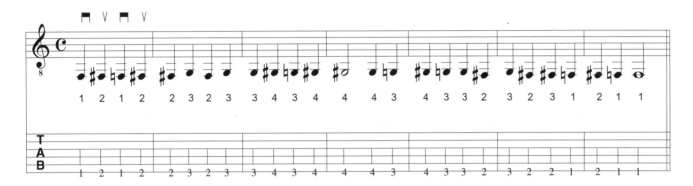

Exercise 15

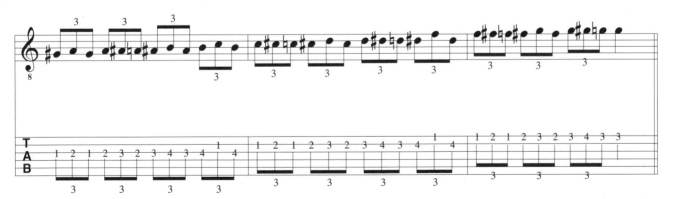

- Accurate timing of triplets is dependent on well-synchronised fretted and strumming hands

- It is important to use regular alternate up- and down-strokes. If you don't, the notes will sound uneven and lumpy

- Begin by pratising slowly with a metronome, and gradually increase the speed

- Start by isolating individual passages, and gradually incorporate more of the fretboard into your practice regime

Tips

Finger independence and synchronisation

Exercise 16

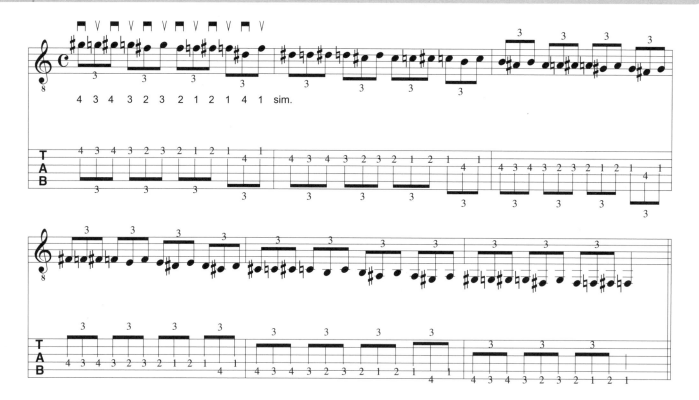

Exercise 17

Exercise 18

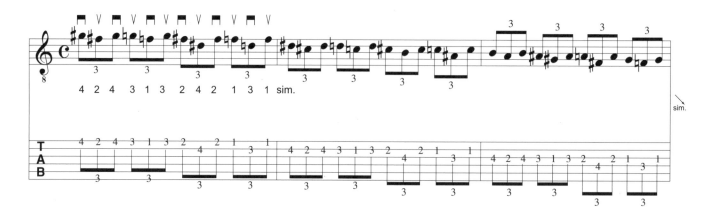

20

Until now, we've only played single notes in one way: using a pick to hit the string concerned. There are other ways to play single notes, including the hammer-on and pull-off. First, we will examine the hammer-on. The concept of the hammer-on is fairly simple and is notated in tablature using an **H**.

1. Pick the first note using the plectrum

2. Play the second note without re-picking by hitting your finger firmly and rapidly onto the string. (N.B. the second note is always on a higher fret). If you do this with enough force, the second note should sound, even though you didn't re-pick it. If you didn't put your finger on the string accurately enough, or with enough force, all that probably happened was the first note stopped ringing. Try repeating the exercise, and keep doing so, until the second note rings out clearly.

The following exercises will help you to practise slurs using this technique.

Single hammer-ons (TAB=H)

The high E and B strings are particularly useful for practising the hammer-on technique because the thinner strings make it easier to achieve the right effect. It is important that the finger meets the string with the middle of the fingertip and that you hit the centre of the fret. This is the optimum position for playing the note.

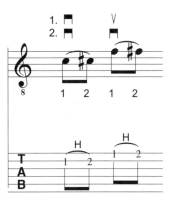

Practise the exercises in two ways:

1. Using alternating up- and down-strokes ⊓ V

2. Using only down-strokes ⊓

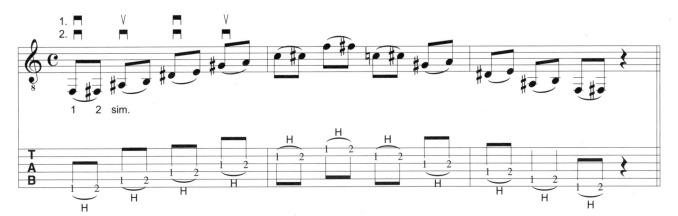

- To practice the hammer-ons it might help you to count out loud on each plectrum stroke, e.g. 'one', 'two'

- Both plectrum strokes should be even

- Isolate any problematic passages and practise them separately.

- Practicing with a metronome will help you keep a regular tempo

- To start with, only practise the pattern in the suggested area of the fretboard

- Record your practice sessions. By listening back to what you have played you will learn where you are going wrong

Tips

The hammer-on

Double hammer-on

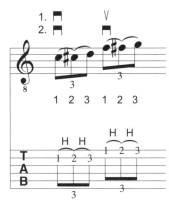

The double hammer-on works on the same principle as the single hammer-on, but instead allows you to play two hammered-on notes for every one note that you pick. Use the same technique as for the single hammer-on but repeat step two for the third note.

In this case, the sound for the final two triplet quavers stems from the first note.

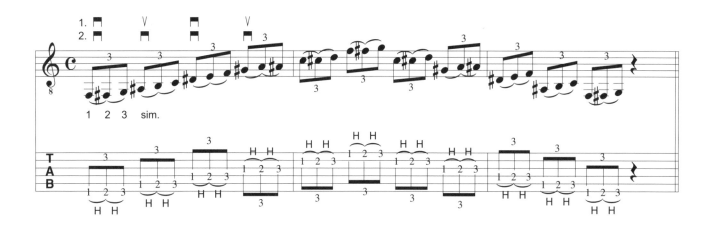

Triple hammer-on

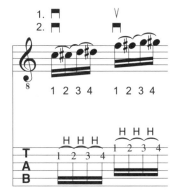

The triple hammer-on also works on the same principle as the single hammer on, but allows you to play three notes for every one note that you pick. Use the same technique as for the single hammer-on but repeat step two for the third and fourth notes.

In this case, the sound for the final three semiquavers stems from the first note.

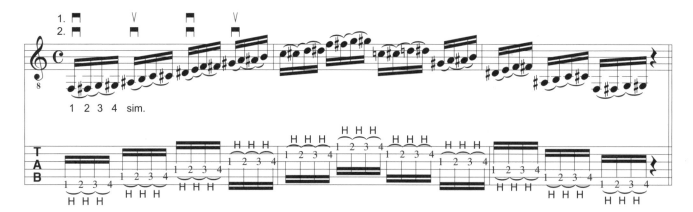

The pull-off can be thought of as the opposite of a hammer-on. It is performed as follows and is notated in tablature using a **P**.

1. Pick the first note.

2. Remove your third finger from the string. As you do this, make a slight downwards pulling motion with your finger. This should cause the note your first finger is fretting to ring out. The first few times you try it, the string may stop ringing as you remove your finger. Make sure you don't hit the string below!

When playing pull-offs on the e' string, be sure not to move you finger too far away from the fretboard, or you may find your ability to play fast passages is compromised.

The pull-off is a good way of slurring two notes. The following exercises will help you to practise slurs using this technique.

Single pull-offs (TAB=P)

The high E and B strings are particularly useful for practising the simple pull-off technique because the thinner strings make it easier to achieve the right effect.

Practise the exercises in two ways:

1. using alternating up- and down-strokes

2. using only down-strokes

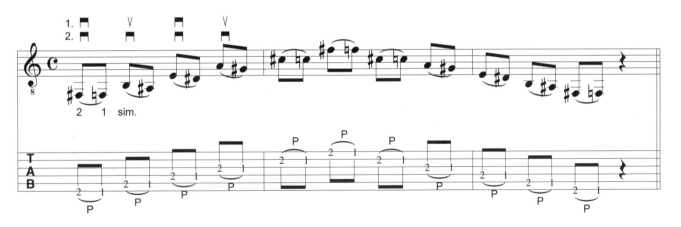

- To practise the pull-offs it might help you to count out loud on each plectrum stroke, i.e. 'one', 'two'

- Both plectrum strokes should be even

- Isolate any problematic passages and practise them separately. Practising with a metronome will help you keep a regular tempo

- To start with, only practise the pattern in the suggested area of the fretboard

- Record your practice sessions. By listening back to yourself you will learn where you are going wrong

Tips

The pull-off

Double pull-off

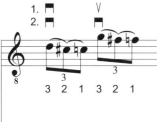

The double pull-off works on the same principle as the single pull-off, but allows you to play three notes for every one note that you pick. Use the same technique as for the single pull-off but repeat step two for the third note.

The sound for the final two triplets stems from the first note.

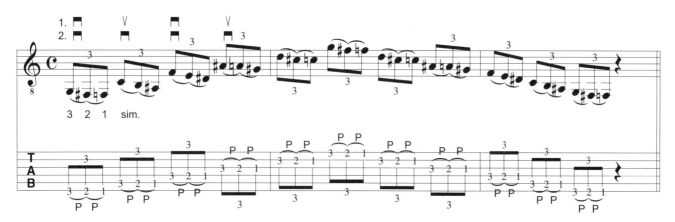

Triple pull-off

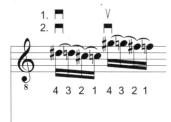

The triple pull-off also works on the same principle as the single pull-off, but allows you to play three notes for every one note that you pick. Use the same technique as for the single pull-off but repeat step two for the third and fourth notes.

The sound for the final three semiquavers stems from the first note.

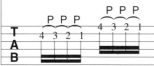

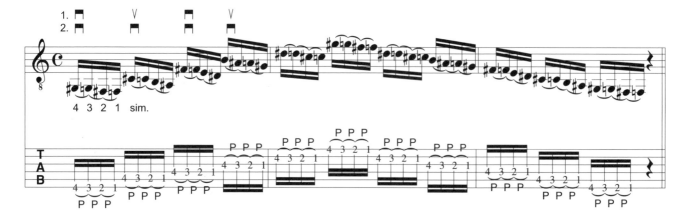

Once you've mastered the simple hammer-ons and pull-offs, you can start to try playing things that combine multiple hammer-ons and pull-offs. The following exercises will help you to do this. Exercises 31 and 32 begin with a combination of up- and down-strokes.

Mastering the single hammer-on and pull-off is essential before embarking on these exercises.

Once you are able to play the exercises on this page using the suggested fingerings, you can also practise them using the ring finger and little finger.

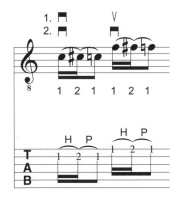

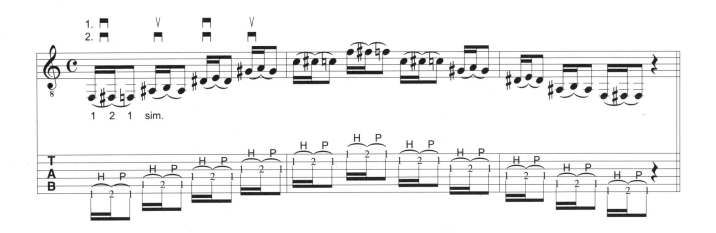

This exercise is a reversal of the previous. Here, the pull-off precedes the hammer-on. Practise the example on the right to begin with, and once you can play this, move on to the complete exercise.

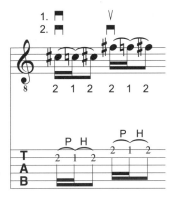

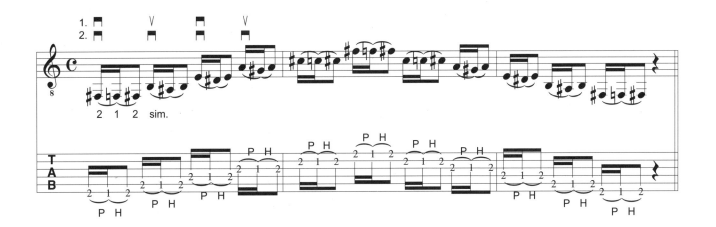

Combined hammer-ons/pull-offs

Double hammer-on/one pull-off

Now that you can play combined single hammer-ons and pull-offs, it is time to work on combining the double and triple varieties. In the same way as before, the sound for the final three semiquavers stems from the first note.

The main challenge with a double hammer-on followed by a pull-off is achieving both a consistent tempo and a consistent level of sound. This exercise, therefore, is best rehearsed with a metronome.

Recommended tempo: ♪=60

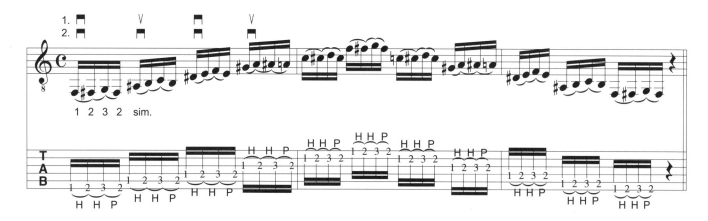

Double pull-off/one hammer-on

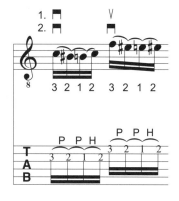

This is a reversal of the previous exercise. Make sure your pull-offs are equal in volume to the hammer-on. In the same way as the previous exercise, the main challenge here is consistency.

Recommended tempo: ♪=60

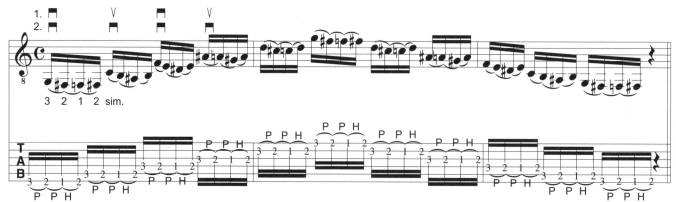

26

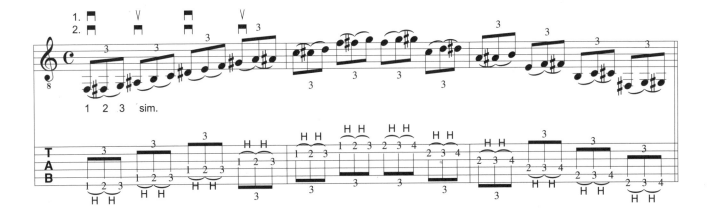

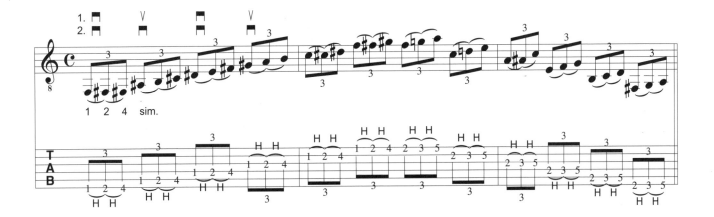

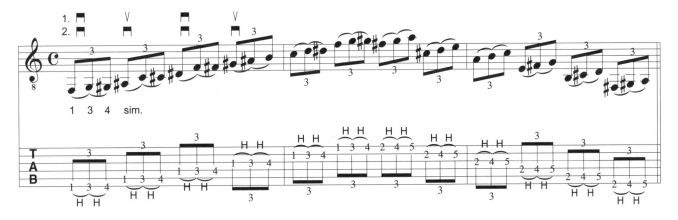

- First, make sure you can play the relevant finger-pattern. If you have difficulty, practise the figure slowly on each string

- Once you are comfortable with the finger-pattern, practise the double hammer-ons

- Start by isolating individual passages, then gradually incorporate more of the fretboard into your practice regime

Tips

Exercises

Exercise 22: pull-offs using all six strings. Variation 2

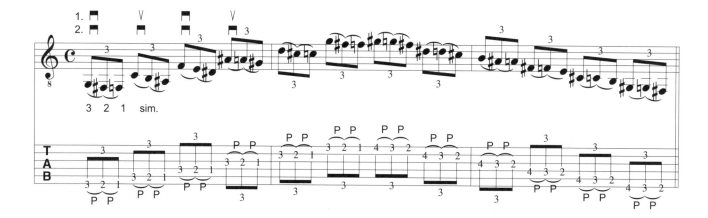

Exercise 23: pull-offs using all six strings. Finger-pattern 4–2–1. Variation 2

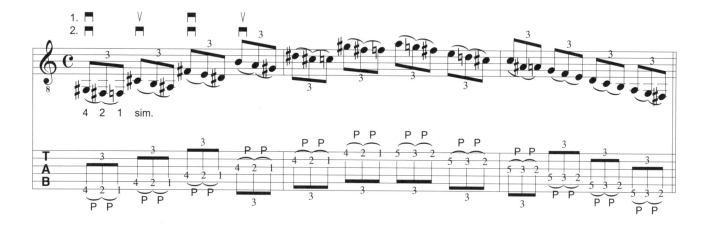

Exercise 24: pull-offs using all six strings. Finger-pattern 4–3–1. Variation 2

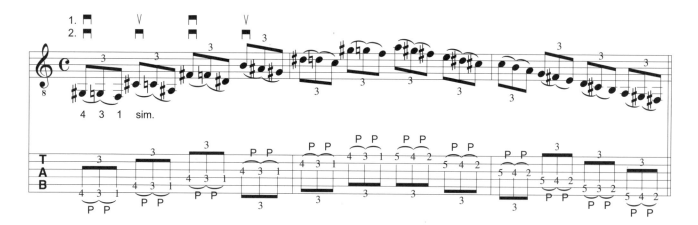

Tips

- First, make sure you can play the relevant finger-pattern. If you have difficulty, practise the figure slowly on each string

- Once you feel comfortable with the finger-pattern, practise the double pull-offs

- Start by isolating individual passages, then gradually incorporate more of the fretboard into your practice regime

A trill is a rapid alternation between two different notes, usually a tone or a semitone apart. The following exercises will help you learn how to play trills. To start with, the rhythm is written as a group of four semiquavers. Start at a slow speed and gradually increase it until you are going as fast as you can!

- Exercises 25–27 begin with a hammer-on
- Exercise 28 begins with a pull-off

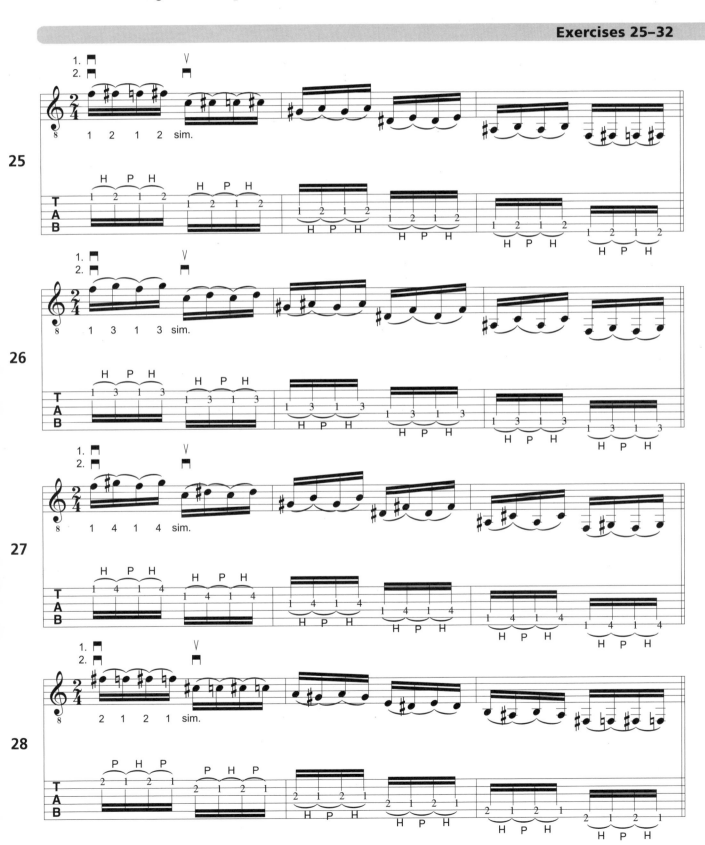

Trills

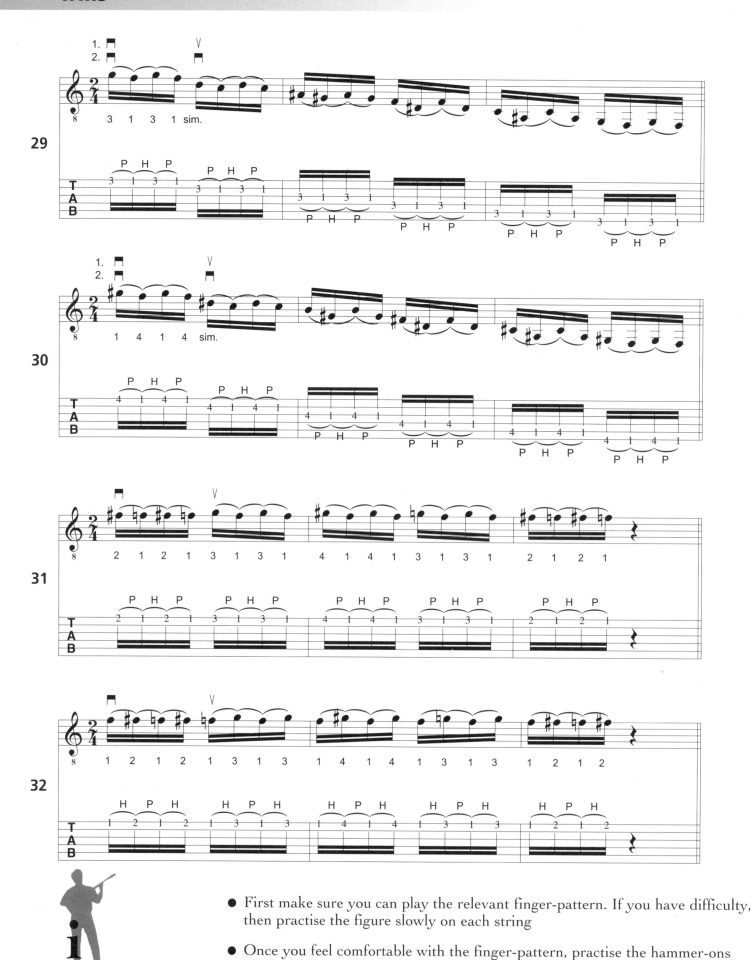

- First make sure you can play the relevant finger-pattern. If you have difficulty, then practise the figure slowly on each string

- Once you feel comfortable with the finger-pattern, practise the hammer-ons and pull-offs

Tips

Symbol	Explanation
▀	Down-stroke
V	Up-stroke
𝄞 8	The 8 under the treble clef indicates that the guitar sounds one octave lower than notated
T A B	Tablature sign. In tablature, the six strings are depicted using lines. The lowest indicates the low E string, the uppermost the high E string
3 / 10	A number on the line indicates at which fret and on what string a note should be played. Here: tenth fret = A string and third fret = b string
1 2 3 4	Fingering for the fretted hand: 1 = index finger, 2 = middle finger, 3 = ring finger, 4 = little finger
sim.	Simile (in the same manner)
H	Hammer-on
P	Pull-off
FR	Finger-roll
sim.	The specified section should be played forwards then backwards in the same manner
sim.	The specified section should be played backwards then forwards in the same manner
sim.	The specified section should be played forwards in the same manner
sim.	The specified section should be played backwards in the same manner

Glossary of terms used

Name	Description
Down-stroke	Downward stroke with the plectrum
Pull-off	The first note is picked, the second is plucked by the finger of the fretted hand
Quaver	Note value: there are eight quavers in a 4/4 bar
Right/left hand	The hand which does the picking. If you're right-handed use your right hand and if you're left-handed use your left hand
Hammer-on	The first note is picked, the second is produced by slapping the finger of the fretted hand onto the string
Up-stroke	Upwards stroke with the plectrum
Fret	Metal strips separating the frets. (Standard = 22 frets, also 19, 21, 24)
Finger-roll	By 'rolling' the finger, it moves to play the neighbouring string
Fingering	Fretted hand finger sequence e.g. 1–2–3–4
Left/right hand	The hand which frets the notes: if you're right-handed use your left hand and if you're left-handed use your right hand
Position	The position indicates the location of the fretted hand. Index finger on the first fret=first position
Changing position	If the index finger moves up or down the fretboard, this is known as changing position
Metronome	Pulse generator. Acoustic or electronic sounds indicate between 40 and 208 beats per minute
Pick, Plectrum	Piece of metal, plastic or wood used to play the strings
String jumping	The act of jumping over one or more strings with the plectrum
Semiquaver	Note value: four semiquavers make one crotchet
Synchronisation	Synchronising the fretted and picking hands
Tablature	Guitar notation using numbers on six lines which represent the strings: 3 = third fret
Trill	Alternation of two notes by playing them in rapid succession
Triad	A two-part note is split into three parts: a quaver triplet (three quavers) has the same value as two quavers
Crotchet	Note value. Four crotchets together make a 4/4 bar
Alternate picking	Alternating strokes with the plectrum. Up- and down-strokes are alternated